JFK
CONSPIRACIES

JFK
CONSPIRACIES

First published in the UK in 2013

© Demand Media Limited 2013

www.demand-media.co.uk

Printed and bound in China

ISBN 978-1-909217-32-4

The views in this book are those of the author but they are general views only and
readers are urged to consult the relevant and qualified specialist for individual
advice in particular situations.

Demand Media Limited hereby exclude all liability to the extent permitted by law
of any errors or omissions in this book and for any loss, damage or expense
(whether direct or indirect) suffered by a third party relying on any information
contained in this book.

All our best endeavours have been made to secure copyright clearance for every
photograph used but in the event of any copyright owner being overlooked
please address correspondence to Demand Media Limited, Waterside
Chambers, Bridge Barn Lane, Woking, Surrey, GU21 6NL

Contents

Introduction

The assassination of John F Kennedy is one of the defining moments of the 1960s, and one of the most shocking events of modern times. The young president was popular, rich and had already racked up notable political successes at home and abroad: he had taken on the Russians over the division of Berlin and during the Cuban Missile Crisis; he had challenged his country to land a man on the moon by the end of the decade; and he had brought civil rights and the issues surrounding racial segregation to the forefront of domestic politics. But he had also overseen the botched landing at the Bay of Pigs in Cuba, angered the mob by clamping down on organised crime and upset many within his own party by causing a rift with Vice-President Lyndon Johnson.

Kennedy was born to Joseph and Rose in Brookline, Massachusetts, in May 1917. The family was of Irish descent, with all eight of his great-grandparents having emigrated from Ireland. He lived in Brookline until he was ten, when the family moved to the Bronx. He spent his childhood summers at Hyannisport and the winters at the family home in Palm Beach, Florida.

When he was 14 he joined his older brother, Joe Jr, at the Choate School in Connecticut but he spent several years in Joe's shadow and developed a rebellious streak that often got him into trouble. He first travelled abroad in 1935 to study

Above: *The Kennedy Family at Hyannisport, with John at the rear left*

at the London School of Economics but ill health forced him to return to the United States. Indeed, Kennedy was beset by health problems his entire life.

He almost died from scarlet fever in 1920 and immediately contracted measles, whooping cough, chicken pox and frequent respiratory infections. He was an active sportsman at school and university and picked up countless injuries, and he was then diagnosed with colitis, Addison's disease (lack of function in the adrenal glands), which almost killed him in 1947, and poor thyroid function. He also suffered from chronic back pain and underwent major surgery, but he eventually concealed the problem by wearing a brace. He took

JFK **CONSPIRACIES**

steroids, iodine, cortisone, testosterone and a variety of medication throughout his adult life but he managed to keep his health problems from making the headlines because he doubted that America would elect a sick man to public office.

Kennedy travelled throughout Europe for his university thesis in the late 1930s. He returned to London on September 1st 1939, the day Germany invaded Poland and plunged Europe into war. The Kennedy family was in the House of Commons for Britain's declaration of war two days later, and John helped repatriate the American survivors of the SS *Athenia*, which had been torpedoed. He completed his 'Appeasement in Munich' thesis the following year before graduating from Harvard. He then enrolled at the Stanford School of Business.

Kennedy wasn't fit enough to join the army because of his ongoing back problems so he enlisted as an ensign in the navy in September 1941. He was serving under the Secretary of the Navy when the Japanese attacked Pearl Harbor and he immediately signed up to command a torpedo patrol boat. While performing night operations in

the Solomon Islands in August 1943, Kennedy's PT-109 was rammed and sunk by the Japanese destroyer *Amagiri*. Kennedy took a vote on whether the surviving crewmen should surrender or swim to safety. They decided to escape and Kennedy, despite a recurrence of his back injury, towed a wounded crewman to a nearby island. When they were rescued, Kennedy was awarded the Navy & Marine Corps Medal. He received

Above: *Kennedy on his navy patrol boat*

Far Left: *John F Kennedy*

Above: *President Kennedy meets Soviet Premier Nikita Khrushchev in 1961*

immediately hospitalised with more spinal problems that saw him sidelined for much of the next two years.

At the Democratic National Convention in 1956 he was nominated for vice-president but he finished second in the balloting, a vote that pleased his father because he didn't believe John's Catholicism or the strength of the Eisenhower camp would have given him much exposure. Four years later, Joe Sr knew the time was right to campaign for the presidency. John faced challenges from Hubert Humphrey and Wayne Morse but he saw them both off and gave his famous 'New Frontier' speech that challenged the American people. He then overcame opposition from Lyndon Johnson and Adlai Stevenson, and, by July, had secured his party's nomination as their presidential candidate.

Kennedy knew he needed popular support in the south so he asked Johnson to be his vice-presidential candidate. He also knew he had to address the issues of Cuba and Russia, how to stimulate the stagnating economy, promoting the American space program, as well civil rights, racial inequality and his own religious background.

In the latter half of 1960 Kennedy

an honourable discharge in 1945 and, through his father's connections, covered the Potsdam Conference as a journalist for William Randolph Hearst's newspaper.

After the war, which had claimed the life of his older brother, John was encouraged by his father to run for congress. He won the Democratic 11th District in Massachusetts and served for the next six years. He then defeated Republican Henry Lodge for the US Senate seat in 1952. He married Jacqueline the following year but was

took part in the first televised presidential debates opposite Republican Richard Nixon. Whereas those listening on the radio thought the debates were closely fought and that Nixon probably shaded them, TV viewers were more impressed with Kennedy's appearance and demeanour (Nixon wasn't clean shaven and seemed to perspire nervously). The Kennedy campaign gained momentum and he eventually defeated Nixon in one of the closest elections in history.

He was sworn in at the end of January 1961 and he ended the inauguration with his famous rallying cry: "Ask not what your country can do for you, ask what you can do for your country." He also asked the countries of the world to unite

Above: *Chief Justice Earl Warren administers the oath of office to Kennedy in January 1961*

against their common enemies: tyranny, poverty, disease and war.

The first weeks of his presidency were spent dismantling the Eisenhower regime and there was certainly some confusion in the White House about who was doing which job, but Kennedy was happy to take quick and difficult decisions on tax reforms, federal funding for education, medical care for the elderly, and assigning economic aid to deprived rural areas. He also promised to tackle racial segregation and human rights. He was particularly successful in turning the recession into a period of substantial growth – during which car sales rose by 40% and industrial output by 15% – and he also lobbied to have the death penalty abolished. He also laid down a challenge to NASA and the people of America to put a man on the Moon before the end of the decade. His advisors warned him that such an undertaking would be prohibitively expensive but, when the Russians launched Yuri Gagarin into space in April 1961, the US realised it could be left behind in both the space race and the race to develop long-range ballistic missiles. Kennedy initially asked the Soviets to join the Apollo program but Krushchev refused lest he give away vital information regarding their nuclear weapon delivery systems.

Kennedy's foreign policy would be dominated by the Cold War. He initially reacted angrily to Krushchev and viewed his speeches as personal challenges, and the Soviet Premier left their meetings believing Kennedy to be intelligent but easily bullied. Kennedy felt so threatened by the Soviets when they erected the Berlin Wall to stop East Berliners fleeing west that he committed more than three billion dollars to the defence budget and recruited 200,000 troops. When he spoke of an attack on West Berlin being a direct attack on the US, his approval rating reached 85%.

Although he bolstered his public appearance with powerful speeches, in private Kennedy was often indecisive on matters of global importance. He was concerned that Cuba gave the Russians a foothold in the West, he knew there was growing opposition to the Vietnam War, he believed his country was being eroded from within by organised crime, and this supposed beacon of hope was being undermined by racial inequality and a poor record on civil rights.

Then everything changed on one day in Dallas.

The Death of a President

There are many theories as to who was responsible for gunning down the 35th American President, but the proponents do at least agree on most of the facts leading up to the shooting on November 22nd 1963.

Kennedy, Vice-President Johnson and Texas Governor John Connally discussed a potential visit to Dallas in June 1963. Their aims were to raise Democratic Party funds for the re-election campaign in 1964 and to build political bridges with the people of a state that had largely voted against Kennedy in 1960.

The trip was formally announced in September, but the exact itinerary and the route the motorcade would take through Dallas weren't divulged until mid-November. Fearful of the public's reaction to Kennedy – UN Ambassador Adlai Stevenson was jeered and spat at during his visit – he was advised not to make the trip, but the president would not be deterred and the police undertook the biggest security operation in the city's history.

On Thursday 21st November, Kennedy made a speech dedicating the Brooks Air Force Base's school of aerospace medicine. He then enjoyed a testimonial dinner in Houston honouring Congressman Albert Thomas, after which he flew to the Texas Hotel in Fort Worth. The following morning, he made a breakfast speech to the Chamber of Commerce in the hotel ballroom. He

Left: *Kennedy in Fort Worth on the morning of his assassination*

and wife Jacqueline then made the short flight to Love Field in Dallas aboard Air Force One.

The presidential motorcade comprised a lead car, an unmarked Ford carrying Dallas Police Chief Jesse Curry; the president's 1961 Lincoln Continental; a follow-up car with more security personnel; the vice-president's car and security; plus two press cars. It left the airfield for the journey through downtown Dallas to the Trade Mart building at around 11.40am. The motorcade stopped twice so that Kennedy could shake hands with well-wishers before turning right onto Main Street.

The streets in the city centre were packed with people hoping to catch a glimpse of Kennedy with Jackie but there were no problems reported on the route. At 12.29pm, the motorcade turned right onto Houston Street before slowing to below ten miles an

hour and turning sharp left onto Elm Street beneath the Texas School Book Depository in Dealey Plaza. A few moments later, shots echoed around the plaza. Kennedy was struck in his upper back and in the head.

Secret Service Agent Clint Hill ran from the car behind and leaped onto the rear of the presidential limousine to try to shield the stricken president but he was too late. A piece of skull about the

size of his palm was missing from above Kennedy's right ear, and the limousine was covered in brain matter and blood.

The motorcade immediately accelerated under the triple underpass at the western end of the plaza. Hill almost fell off the rear of the car but he eventually managed to force Jacqueline back into her seat. As they raced towards Parkland Memorial Hospital, Hill also noticed that Governor Connally appeared to have

Above: *Bill and Gayle Newman try to protect their children during the shooting. The grassy knoll is in the background*

Far Left: *The presidential limousine on Main Street moments before the shooting*

THE DEATH OF A PRESIDENT

Above: *Ike Altgens's rare picture, taken between the second and third shots, shows Governor Connally turned to his right and Kennedy's hands up to his throat*

Centre: *The Texas School Book Depository in Dealey Plaza*

been struck in the chest.

When they arrived at the hospital, Special Agent Winston Lawson ran inside and returned with orderlies and two gurneys. Connally was helped onto one but Jackie Kennedy would not let go of her husband's head until Hill covered him with his coat. There was pandemonium in the hospital as doctors rushed the mortally wounded president into trauma room one while the press and public clamoured for news of his condition.

Attorney General Robert Kennedy was immediately put in touch with Clint Hill and the agent had to inform him that the situation for his brother was extremely grim. Two priests were called to administer the last rites and Kennedy was pronounced dead at one o'clock. Doctor Earl Rose knew that a homicide in the county meant that he would perform the autopsy at Parkland Hospital, but the Secret Service had

Above: *Secret Service Agent Clint Hill leaps onto the back of the presidential limousine as it accelerates towards Parkland Memorial Hospital*

already acquired a coffin and told him they were taking the body back to Washington for autopsy.

Lyndon Johnson was already on his way back to Love Field when Jackie left the hospital with her husband's body. Barely three hours after arriving in Dallas, Air Force One left for Washington. During the flight, Johnson was sworn in as the 36th president while Jackie, still wearing her bloodstained pink dress, stood at his side.

Back in Dealey Plaza, the police had already searched the book depository and found three spent shell casings by the sixth floor window. Deputy Eugene Boone had also recovered a rifle from the northwest corner of the building on the same floor.

Who fired at the president and why has divided opinion and a nation ever since, and there are several candidates with the means, motive and opportunity to carry out the assassination.

KENNEDY

REPORT

WALL ST. EDITION
LATEST PRICES

Journal

IS SHOT,
D DEAD

rk

American

7TH SPORTS
RACING
☆ ☆ ☆ ☆ ☆ ☆ ☆
SPORTS EXTRA

19

Lee Harvey Oswald

Oswald was born in New Orleans in 1939, but his mother, Marguerite, moved the family to Dallas when he was five. He went to school in the local area but was labelled as only having average intelligence and was often described by teachers and classmates as withdrawn and temperamental. His spelling and writing were extremely poor, possibly due to dyslexia, which may also have contributed to his IQ of only 103 (this may not have been due to low intelligence after all but because he found reading and answering the questions difficult and time-consuming). He found solace in reading privately, however, and devoured hundreds of books.

In 1952 the family moved to New York but Oswald apparently threatened his half-brother's wife with a knife. He was also having problems at school and a psychological evaluation at a juvenile reformatory claimed he created a vivid fantasy life to compensate for his intellectual and physical inadequacy. His poor behaviour gradually improved with guidance, however, and Marguerite took him back to New Orleans in 1954. His interest in Communism stemmed from when he was handed a flyer about Julius and Ethel Rosenberg who had been executed as Soviet spies at Sing Sing prison in 1953.

The following year Oswald dropped out of school and took a low-paid

LEE HARVEY OSWALD AS A MARINE

COMMISSION EXHIBIT No. 2894

Above: *The apartment building in Minsk where Oswald lived after his defection to the Soviet Union*

Left: *A Warren Commission photo of Oswald*

position as a desk clerk but, when his mother relocated them to Fort Worth, he went back to school. He dropped out again, however, and joined the marines aged 17 to train in radar operations. In 1957 he was cleared to work with confidential files as no worrying background information on him had surfaced, this despite the fact that he was overtly pro-Castro and was alienating colleagues with his extreme views. He was posted to El Toro in California and then Atsugi in Japan.

His excellent initial shooting scores saw him reach the rank of sharpshooter but further tests saw him drop back to marksman. He was court-martialled twice, once for discharging an unauthorised handgun into his own elbow and again for fighting with the sergeant who punished him. Then, having inexplicably fired his weapon into the jungle from his sentry post in the Philippines, he was demoted to the

Mannlicher- Carcano Rifle
Commission Exhibit 139
FBI Exhibit C14

Above: *The Carcano rifle bought by Oswald*

rank of private.

During his time with the marines he continued to read. Amongst the piles of books he'd accumulated, several were of a socialist nature, and he applied to the Young People's Socialist League claiming to be a Marxist. He also tried to teach himself Russian, although his exam results were poor.

In September 1959 Oswald received a hardship discharge from the marines by claiming his mother needed care. He had some money saved so he used it to travel via France, Britain and Finland to the Soviet Union. He only had a short-term tourist visa but he used his time to try to convince his guide and several low-ranking Russian officials that he wanted to defect. No one could understand why an American with reasonable prospects in the West would want to become a Russian citizen and

his application was refused. Oswald made a half-hearted attempt to slit his wrists so the Soviets kept him under observation in a psychiatric unit until the end of October.

Oswald then went to the US embassy to inform them that he intended to pass classified information to the Soviets, which was reported in several newspapers in the United States. Oswald was allowed to stay because the Americans didn't believe he knew anything of interest, but, instead of being put to work at Moscow University, Oswald was recruited as a lathe operator in Minsk. He was paid well and lived in a comfortable apartment, but he was under 24-hour surveillance and this wasn't what he'd been expecting.

By 1961 Oswald had grown bored of his job and the dreary surroundings so he applied to move back to the US

Left: *A Smith & Wesson Model 10 of the type used to kill Officer Tippit*

with his new bride, Marina Prusakova, and their young daughter, June. The Russians had realised that he had never been a CIA operative and didn't know any sensitive information, and he was not sufficiently skilled to be moulded into a Russian agent either so they let him go. When he returned to America, Oswald was expecting, indeed hoping, to become a media sensation but he was completely ignored. He worked briefly as a welder and an apprentice print technician but he was apparently rude to co-workers and insufferably arrogant. His love of Russian literature also caused friction amongst his colleagues and he left soon afterwards.

Seemingly disillusioned with life and feeling unimportant and anonymous, Oswald bought an Italian 6.5mm Carcano Model 91/38 bolt-action rifle and a Smith & Wesson .38 revolver by mail order using the alias A. Hidell. (The rifle is sometimes incorrectly called a Mannlicher-Carcano but Mannlicher was actually the name of the rimless ammunition cartridge.) On the night of April 10th 1963 Oswald shot at retired Major-General Edwin Walker – a vehement anti-Communist

LEE HARVEY OSWALD

Right: *Oswald poses with the rifle used in the Walker assassination attempt*

Far Right: *Major-General Edwin A Walker*

and segregationist who had a growing following in the south – while the general was at home in his office. The bullet struck the window frame and Walker survived with minor injuries to his arm.

(There were no suspects in this shooting until after the Kennedy assassination when Oswald's name was suggested. Marina Oswald testified to the Warren Commission, which was investigating the murder, that her husband believed Walker to be a fascist and that he'd confessed to the attempt on the general's life on the night in question. She hadn't said anything at the time because Oswald was beating her and she feared for her life. The bullet found in Walker's office was too badly damaged for most forensic tests but neutron activation analysis – a process for assessing the concentrations of various elements in the atomic nucleus – later concluded that it was extremely likely the bullet was made by the same manufacturer and fired by the same rifle as that used in the Kennedy assassination.)

Oswald returned to New Orleans and joined the Reily Coffee Company as a machine greaser but he was soon fired for laziness. He then decided to set up a Fair Play for Cuba office and began distributing leaflets backing Fidel Castro. He also tried to infiltrate and disrupt several anti-Castro groups. He was later confronted by anti-Castro militant Carlos Bringuier, and both men were arrested for disturbing the peace after a scuffle. While in custody, Oswald asked to speak with the FBI and he spent an hour with John Quigley.

A week later, Oswald was back distributing leaflets in front of the cameras. He was asked to take part in a radio debate with Carlos Bringuier and accepted. He then tried to convince his wife to help him hijack a plane to Cuba but Marina was pregnant with their second child and thought the plan ridiculous. Soon afterwards, Oswald was on the move again, this time by bus from Houston to Mexico City. Once there, he applied for a transit visa to the Soviet Union via Cuba. He was initially refused but, after several arguments, he was given permission to enter Cuba. He declined and returned instead to Dallas by bus at the beginning of October.

With his life seemingly going nowhere, he applied for a job at the Texas School Book Depository two weeks

building if the FBI didn't stop bothering his wife, but Special Agent James Hosty denied the threat was serious and that Oswald merely wanted to report their behaviour as inappropriate.

Just before Kennedy arrived in Dallas, the motorcade route was announced: it passed directly in front of the book depository. On November 21st, Oswald asked Frazier for a lift to Irving so he could collect some curtain rods. The following morning they returned to Dallas. Oswald left $170 and his wedding ring with Marina but he did carry a parcel to work. He also apparently turned up to the depository with a long, heavy package. Witness stories vary considerably but Oswald was seen by several co-workers on the first floor of the depository in the hour before the shooting. Charles Givens testified to the Warren Commission that he saw Oswald on the sixth floor at 11.55am but he didn't mention this to the police immediately after the assassination.

Ninety seconds after the shooting Oswald was spotted in the second-floor lunchroom by police officer Marrion Baker. Baker drew his gun and approached Oswald but building

Above: *Oswald hands out 'Hands Off Cuba' leaflets*

later and was accepted. He occasionally roomed in Dallas under the alias O. H. Lee and often commuted to work with Wesley Frazier. The following week, Marina bore Oswald a second daughter but the couple were unhappy and spent little time together. Interest in the family suddenly increased, however, with the FBI suspecting Marina of being a Russian spy. Oswald knew they were hassling her so he left a note with a receptionist at the police department. The receptionist claimed it said that Oswald was threatening to blow up the

NEW ORLEANS, LA.
112 723
8   9   63

manager Roy Truly intervened and said that Oswald worked at the depository. Neither man thought Oswald looked in the least bit flustered and he was allowed to leave the building by the front entrance. When more witnesses came forward to say that they had heard shots from the sixth floor and Oswald was the only employee missing, the police were instructed to hunt for a white male around 30 years old standing 5'10" with a slender build.

At 12.40pm Oswald boarded a bus but disembarked after two blocks to take a taxi to his room on North Beckley Avenue. His housekeeper claimed Oswald only stayed for a few minutes before going outside to wait for another bus. When one didn't arrive, he walked a mile to the corner of Tenth and Patton. A few minutes later, Oswald was approached by Dallas Patrolman J D Tippit who had heard the description of the man wanted in connection with the assassination. Tippit pulled up alongside Oswald and spoke to him briefly. As soon as he climbed out of his car, Tippit was shot three times. As he lay in the road, Oswald fired a fourth shot at his head.

Several witnesses heard the shooting

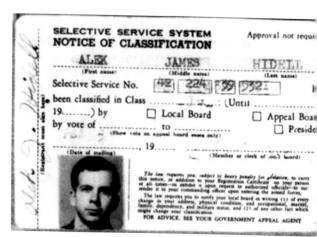

and saw a man running from the scene with a gun. Johnny Brewer, a shoe-shop employee, noticed Oswald acting suspiciously and he notified a ticket clerk at the Texas Theatre after he saw Oswald slip in without paying. The clerk called the police and they arrived at the theatre at 1.45pm.

Officer Nick McDonald waited for the lights to be brought up before approaching Oswald on the upper balcony. Oswald appeared to be ready to surrender but he suddenly removed a revolver from his trousers and aimed at McDonald. The officer managed to jam his thumb between the hammer

Above: One of Oswald's fake ID cards. He used this one to order the rifle and revolver

Far Left: Oswald is led from the Texas Theatre after his capture

Above: *J.D. Tippit*

before Oswald was finally disarmed and led from the theatre.

He was immediately taken to the police department and questioned about the Tippit shooting by Jim Leavelle. When Captain J W Fritz heard who they had in custody, he recognized him as the man missing from the book depository and Oswald was booked for both murders. Despite their best efforts at keeping Oswald away from the press, the police couldn't stop him answering questions as he was transported around the building. Oswald denied shooting Kennedy and claimed he hadn't been charged with the murder.

Oswald was questioned several times over the next two days but he stuck to the curtain-rod story, that he'd been eating lunch when found by Baker and Truly in the depository, and that he didn't own a rifle or revolver despite being presented with photos of him holding them (he claimed the pictures were faked and that he was a patsy). He also claimed in the interviews to be a Marxist rather than a Communist.

Two days after the shootings, Oswald was being led through the basement of the police department on his way to the county jail by Jim

and the firing pin and the gun did not discharge. Oswald then struck McDonald so the policeman, along with Officer Bob Carroll, retaliated

Leavelle. Leavelle joked with Oswald that if anyone shot at him, he hoped they were as good a shot as Oswald. His words would be prophetic: at 11.20am, Jack Ruby, a nightclub owner and small-time criminal who was known to have links within the police department and with the Mafia, stepped forward and shot Oswald point-blank in the lower left chest. The bullet tore his vena cava and aorta and he was pronounced dead at Parkland Memorial Hospital just after 1pm.

The murder was captured live on television and has given rise to hundreds of conspiracy theories, most of which centre around Ruby silencing Oswald so he couldn't divulge information about organised crime to the police. Ruby maintained until his death in 1967, however, that he had shot Oswald to spare Jackie the agony of sitting through his trial, and because Oswald had killed his president.

The case against Oswald remains convincing: he had bought a Carcano rifle and a revolver in the months before the assassination; he was seen entering the book depository with a long, heavy package on the morning of the shootings; Howard Brennan and Amos Euins were standing on the corner of Houston and Elm and they both saw a man lean out of the sixth floor window and fire at the motorcade; other witnesses heard three shots, and three spent cartridges were found with the gun (which had been hastily hidden among the boxes on the sixth floor) in the depository; the gun and surrounding boxes had Oswald's palm prints on them; the improvised paper bag he'd been seen with that morning was also found near the sniper's nest; more than half of the people in Dealey Plaza said all three shots originated from the book depository; ballistic and forensic analysis of Kennedy's gunshot wounds confirm that the shots were fired from the sixth floor of the depository; a bullet found on Governor Connally's hospital gurney and two fragments from the presidential limousine were matched to the rifle; fibres on the rifle were matched with Oswald's shirt, and his hands had traces of firearms residue on them; Oswald was positively identified by nine independent witnesses as being the killer of J D Tippit; the cartridge cases found at the scene belonged to Oswald's revolver – which was on him when he was arrested – to the exclusion of all other weapons; and his wife, Marina, insisted that she had taken the photos of Oswald with the murder weapons and that the pictures could not have been faked.

Independent investigations into the shooting by the Warren Commission, Attorney General Robert Kennedy, J Edgar Hoover at the FBI, John McCone at the CIA and James Rowley of the Secret Service (amongst others) all concluded that Oswald acted alone and that he was driven by a hatred of his country and its society and an overwhelming desire to be seen and remembered as a great man who achieved a position of consequence.

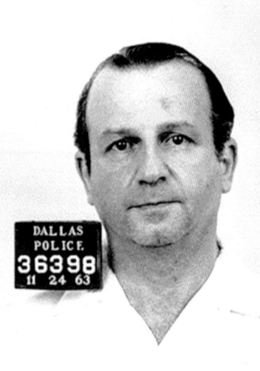

The Warren Commission

In the aftermath of the assassination and the subsequent murder of Lee Harvey Oswald, President Johnson knew he had to provide a concerned public with answers. He appointed Chief Justice Earl Warren to head up the investigation into the shootings so that the truth would be found and that rumours about foreign involvement could be dispelled.

With a nation desperate for answers, the pressure to deliver a comprehensive report within a reasonable timeframe was enormous; the longer it took to investigate, the more time the theories had to evolve. It is a common misconception that the commission conducted its business in secret sessions, but this was not the case. The hearings were closed to the public unless the witness specifically asked to be heard and, although the hearings were conducted in private, they were not secret and no witness was prevented from discussing what had transpired. All witness testimony was then published in full by the commission.

When the report finally came out in September 1964, it said that the shots that had killed Kennedy and injured Governor Connally were fired from the sixth floor of the book depository. It based this assumption on the eyewitness testimony from Brennan and Euins who had seen a man lean out and fire at the motorcade; the fact that the bullet found on Connally's stretcher matched the

Left: *Chief Justice Earl Warren*

THE WARREN COMMISSION

Right: *Earl Warren presents his report to President Johnson in 1964*

JFK **CONSPIRACIES**

Carcano rifle found in the depository to the exclusion of all other weapons; the three used cartridges found in the sniper's nest also matched the rifle; the limousine's windshield was struck on the inside by a bullet fragment; and the nature of the wounds to both men indicated the bullets were fired from above, behind and slightly to the right of the motorcade.

Having thoroughly investigated Oswald's connections with the Soviet Union; the Fair Play for Cuba Committee; the Socialist Workers' Party; the Communist Party, USA; and his meetings with contacts at the Russian and Cuban embassies in Mexico City, the FBI, the CIA, and any other governmental agency, the commission blamed Oswald alone for the assassination.

It cited his deep-rooted resentment of authority, his inability to form close relationships, his rejection of society, his urge to forge a place in history to mask his daily shortcomings and notable failures in civilian life, and his commitment to antagonising the US by declaring himself a Marxist, as his motives for carrying out the assassination, and it also said that the attempt on Walker's life proved that he had the capacity for violence and the mindset of a man capable of killing.

In November 1964, the commission released 26 volumes of documents to support the initial 888-page report. It included the testimony of 552 witnesses and 3,100 exhibits. These records were then transferred to the National Archives, although a small percentage of documents were withheld from the public to serve as 'protection for innocent persons who could otherwise be damaged by their relationship with participants in the case'. (These files were released under the 1966 Freedom of Information Act and the 1992 JFK Records Act. To date, more than 98% of the files have been released, with the only ones still withheld containing confidential tax return information.)

When the initial 888-page Warren Commission report was published in 1964, there was general acceptance from the media but an immediate outcry from the public. Despite the overwhelming evidence, the average American simply didn't believe it was possible for Oswald to have acted alone and a number of alternate theories sprang up.

The conspiracy theorists who believed the report was a whitewash pointed to a host of inconsistencies: a third of all the witnesses in the plaza believed the shots came from the grassy knoll to the front and to the right of the motorcade; seven people claimed to have seen smoke from the stockade fence on the knoll and an eighth said he smelled gunpowder; Gordon Arnold said his cine camera, which had captured the assassination from behind the picket fence on the knoll, was confiscated by two policemen immediately afterwards; some of the president's autopsy photographs have still not been released and several experts claim the photos that *have* been released to the public have been doctored; the limousine was cleaned before detailed forensic analysis could be carried out; many people believe that the first shot to strike Kennedy could not also have been responsible for Governor Connally's injuries, which suggests there were at least two assassins in the plaza; initial police reports submitted by three deputies stated that the weapon found in the depository was a 7.65 Mauser, not a 6.5 Carcano; the House Select Committee on Assassinations concluded that four shots had been fired – with one coming from the grassy knoll – and that acoustic evidence from an open microphone on one of the police motorcycles confirmed

Left: *Attorney General Robert Kennedy*

this; several people claimed at least one shot had been fired from the roof of the neighbouring Dal-Tex Building; former marine colleagues of Oswald thought he was a lousy shot; the rifle had suspect telescopic sights; and several police marksmen could not replicate the three shots in the 5.6 seconds stipulated by the Warren Commission.

More evidence for multiple shooters came from Lee Bowers who was in a railroad tower overlooking the yard behind the grassy knoll. He said he saw two men on the knoll, that one of them was wearing a dark jacket, and that one or more of the shots could have been fired from this position, although the echo meant that he also considered the book depository as being the origin of the shots. The famous film of the assassination taken by Abraham Zapruder appears to show Kennedy's head being snapped back and to the left, which could suggest he was hit by a shot from the front right.

All of these alternatives will be examined in detail later, but we must first go back in time. The evidence against Oswald may be strong (indeed every mock trial conducted since the assassination found him guilty), but a number of organisations also had motives for killing Kennedy, and it is to them that we turn now.

Organised Crime

Since the late 1950s, JFK and his brother, Robert, had been clamping down hard on organised crime. They targeted three Mafia families in particular: Sam Giancana, Godfather of the Chicago area; Johnny Roselli in Las Vegas and Hollywood; and Santo Trafficante Junior in Tampa, who maintained ties with the Cuban underworld and worked closely with Louisiana kingpin Carlos Marcello.

Marcello concerned the Kennedys because he had been born in Tunisia (so was not a citizen) and had taken over the New Orleans crime syndicate. In 1959 he appeared before the senate committee investigating organised crime but he invoked the Fifth Amendment and refused to answer their questions.

The following year Marcello donated half a million dollars to Richard Nixon's presidential campaign fund so he could run against JFK.

When he realised he couldn't indict Marcello, in 1961 Robert Kennedy pressured the immigration authorities to deport him. The CIA abducted and handcuffed him, then bundled him onto an aircraft and forced him to parachute into Central America. Marcello was seething at the apparent loss of dignity so he hired David Ferrie to fly him back into the United States two weeks later. On April 4th Marcello was arrested again and deported to Guatemala, which he claimed was the country of his birth. He returned to Louisiana within

two weeks, however.

By 1962 Marcello had made several threats against Robert Kennedy: "A dog will still bite you if you cut off its tail", and JFK: "Whereas if you cut off the dog's head, the tail will no longer wag". He then told private investigator Edwin Becker that he would have the president killed by someone who would unwittingly take the fall.

There were conflicts of interest, however. These same crime bosses were now working with the CIA to overthrow Castro, although they apparently failed 17 times to eliminate the Cuban prime minister. The embarrassment of the Bay of Pigs invasion gave Castro the excuse to form an alliance with the Russians and bring the Cold War to the West.

The Kennedys decided to change tack and overthrow Castro from within, using his close advisor Juan Almeida to manage the transition under the codename Amworld. A Special Group was set up by Bobby and included Edward Lansdale (Assistant Secretary of Defence for Special Operations) and Secretary Robert McNamara. Its aim was to use espionage, sabotage and other covert tactics to remove the Cuban leader. The date was set for December

1st, 1963.

Bobby tried to keep his brother distanced from the plot and met Cuban exiles in secret. While the CIA assigned agents to the coup, however, it was still working with the Mafia on a number of alternate assassination plans. It was a profitable arrangement because Castro had thrown the mob out of Cuba and his assassination would allow them to restart their gambling and drug smuggling operations out of Havana.

But the CIA had inadvertently revealed the plot to Trafficante, Marcello and Roselli so the Mafia decided to infiltrate the coup. They could also kill JFK in Chicago under the cover of the Amworld operation while continuing to operate in Cuba – where the finger of blame would be pointed when the attempted coup was discovered – when the dust settled. Their deadline was clearly 1st December.

There was increased traffic in communication between mob bosses in October 1963 and the FBI got wind of an assassination attempt. A group of Cubans were discovered with rifles and a plan of Kennedy's route through Chicago, but, instead of arresting them, the FBI placed them under surveillance. But the agents'

cover was blown when the Cubans overheard a radio transmission so they shut up shop.

The FBI had to move so they arrested one of the suspects, Thomas Vallee. He was found with a rifle and 3,000 rounds of ammunition in his car. His new workplace overlooked the motorcade route, and he was a former marine. (He was later released without charge.) Conspiracy theorists point to Vallee being the first patsy lined up by the mob because his background was so similar to Oswald's. The remainder of the president's trip was cancelled – apparently due to the ongoing situation in Vietnam – but that didn't stop the mob trying again.

Four days before his trip to Dallas, Kennedy was in Tampa, Florida, home to Santo Trafficante. Although the Secret Service and local police advised Kennedy against touring in a motorcade – and even tried to dissuade him from going to Tampa at all – Kennedy was rumoured to have a speech planned that Almeida was listening out for in Cuba. The wording was supposed to reassure him that the coup against Castro was going ahead as planned.

Trafficante called off the assassination

Far Left: *Sam Giancana*

attempt by fall guy Gilberto Lopez at the last minute because security was so heavy. This meant the attempt would have to be made in Dallas. Oswald was recruited by Marcello and was in the book depository while the latter was escaping conviction for conspiracy to commit immigration fraud in New Orleans. After the assassination, Trafficante toasted the gunman at a dinner in Tampa. The twelve-fold increase in cases brought against the mob tapered off. (No mention of the Chicago or Tampa events was made in the Warren Commission report because the chief justice was never told by the FBI that a plot to kill Kennedy had been uncovered.)

After the assassination Oswald had to be silenced because the police hadn't killed him. When Jack Ruby shot Oswald while he was being led through the Dallas police station, conspiracy theorists everywhere claimed that the nightclub owner had silenced Oswald on behalf of the mob. So who exactly was Ruby?

Jacob Leon Rubenstein grew up in Chicago in the 1920s. He was a troubled child and spent time in foster homes before being arrested for truancy aged 11 in 1922. When he was released from a juvenile institute he sold racing tip sheets as a part-time bookmaker and worked as an agent for local bin men. He was drafted in 1943 and served as an aircraft mechanic at bases in the US until 1946.

The following year Ruby moved to Dallas, shortened his name and started working in clubs. His staff knew he had a volatile temperament and carried a gun, but he was also known as a wannabe crook who could get things done by intimidation. Many Dallas police officers visited the clubs so Ruby offered them cheap alcohol and private dances from the girls to keep them onside. It also allowed him access to the police stations.

In 1959 Ruby visited a friend, gambler Lewis McWillie, in Cuba. McWillie was a known associate of Mafia boss Santo Trafficante but there's little evidence to suggest Ruby met him. He may, however, have been recruited as a low-level courier to deliver gambling information. Other sources have Ruby smuggling guns to Castro's guerrillas.

The CIA had as much interest in Cuba as the mob. They wanted Castro removed from power so that the Russians didn't have a foothold in the West. And the Mafia wanted their casinos back

in Havana. The two sides formed an uneasy alliance with the goal being to remove Castro. But the Kennedys were completely against the CIA using the mob to eliminate Castro.

On the night of the assassination, Ruby closed the Carousel Club. He was later heard by several of his dancers saying that he would kill Oswald if he got the chance because it would spare Jackie the discomfiture of returning for his trial. Later that night he was seen at police headquarters masquerading as a reporter. It may be that he was already trying to get close to Oswald.

Over the next two days, Ruby's mental state noticeably deteriorated. His sister and friends realised he was unstable but they refused to confront him because of his temper. His housekeeper spoke to him on the morning of Sunday 24th November but said he was not making sense. Two hours later Ruby was asked by one of his dancers to wire her some money so she could meet her rent. He drove to the telegraph office with his dog, left the dog in the car and wired the money at 11.17am. He then walked one block to police headquarters and entered the loading bay a few minutes later (he was well known to the police because most of them frequented his club so he wasn't questioned).

As Oswald was led past, and with the entire event captured on national television, Ruby pulled out his .38 and shot Oswald point blank in the abdomen. In less than 48 hours the country had lost its president and now the man accused of his murder had been silenced by a quick-tempered bruiser with links, however tenuous, to organised crime.

Conspiracy theorists just knew that Oswald had been deliberately silenced, but Ruby vehemently denied any involvement with the mob. He insisted that he had acted alone, which was backed up by those who knew him best, although millions of Americans were now convinced that there had indeed been a conspiracy to assassinate the president. In March 1964, Ruby was sentenced to death for killing Oswald.

In 1985, the case took another twist when Mafia boss Carlos Marcello confessed to being involved in the assassination to FBI informant Jack Van Laningham. Van Laningham had been incarcerated at Texarkana Correctional Penitentiary for bank robbery when he befriended Marcello. To his great

surprise, Marcello confessed to having Kennedy killed because the president's brother, Robert, had launched an all-out assault on organised crime and he'd even gone as far as deporting Marcello to Guatemala. When Marcello returned from exile, he apparently decided to go after the Kennedys.

It was an ill-kept secret that mob money from bootlegged alcohol during Prohibition had made Kennedy's father, Joseph, rich enough to bankroll JFK's presidential campaign. Joe had also reportedly struck a deal with Sam Giancana to help rig the votes in the city's marginal wards so that John would win the Illinois nomination in the traditional swing state. However, once he'd made it into the White House, Joe apparently refused to pay Giancana in full. As the Kennedy brothers were now biting the hand that had fed them, something drastic had to be done, and Giancana vowed that the Mafia would one day get even.

Giancana and Marcello knew they couldn't send a hit squad with machineguns to Dallas because the link to organised crime would be too overt, so they had to have an anonymous patsy carry out the assassination. Marcello

Far Left: *Juan Almeida was supposed to undermine Castro's government from within*

recruited Oswald in the knowledge that the police would shoot him as soon as he was cornered. But things didn't go to plan: Oswald tried to shoot his way out of the movie theatre having killed Tippit but the police didn't shoot back. Now Oswald might be broken during his interrogation, so he had to be silenced. Jack Ruby ran a number of small operations for Marcello but he'd been caught skimming takings and owed the crime boss so he was given a stark choice: eliminate Oswald or be killed himself.

Marcello's confession can only be accurately assessed when the hours of tapes recorded by the radio in Van Laningham's cell are released by the authorities. Until then, it may be the boast of a man proud to have achieved the impossible, or an unreasonable claim for a hit he actually knew nothing about.

Conspiracy theorists like G Robert Blakey believe that Ruby was instructed to close the club so he could go home and be given instructions over the phone. His sister recalled him throwing up in the bathroom after one conversation and alleges this was the moment Carlos Marcello called in the debt. After shooting Oswald, Ruby repeatedly asked the authorities to take him to Washington so he could tell them the full story, but his requests were always denied. In 1967, he succumbed to cancer and his secrets died with him.

While the House Select Committee on Assassinations concluded that Kennedy wasn't killed by a crime syndicate, it could not rule out the possibility that the murder was carried out by individuals with links to organised crime. It was widely accepted that the Mafia, the CIA and anti-Castro Cubans were all trying to overthrow Castro, and they may have teamed up to assassinate Kennedy under the protection of Amworld. Mafia foot-soldier Johnny Roselli had worked with the CIA during their attempts on Castro's life and he provided exact details of the assassination plot, most of which checked out when investigated by reporter Jack Anderson, but he was a trusted confidant of the CIA and had access to some of their information.

There are, however, a number of problems with the mob connection. Who, for example, was supposed to silence Ruby? Also, if the Mafia was linked with the assassination beyond doubt, then Bobby Kennedy would surely have clamped down even harder

Left: *Jack Van Laningham shared a cell with Carlos Marcello and heard him confess to organising the Kennedy assassination*

on organised crime. And was it possible to connect Oswald to organised crime in the first place? The latter question can be answered definitively: Oswald was raised in New Orleans and his uncle was a bookmaker for Carlos Marcello. He was also part of a civil air patrol outfit that included David Ferrie, Marcello's pilot and private investigator. But these connections are tenuous at best and it's unlikely Oswald was recruited by the mob as a patsy.

The Amworld plot to overthrow Cuba is also questionable. It comes from a single document released by the CIA years after the event. Both the Kennedys and the agency were well known for drawing up contingency plans, and there may well have been another attempt to overthrow Castro in the pipeline, but the reality is that John F Kennedy was already communicating indirectly with the Cuban leader, urging him to abandon the Soviets who had not helped deliver the utopia the Cuban people had been promised. For Secretary of Defence Robert McNamara and Kennedy himself to have no knowledge of Amworld meant one of two things: the CIA and mob had successfully shielded the second invasion from them and the military, or the plan hadn't been activated, which meant it didn't really exist at all. The evidence suggests the latter.

The final nail in the coffin for mob involvement in the Kennedy assassination is the fact that, although he was clamping down on their illegal activities, the Mafia needed Kennedy. The crime bosses believed he was still trying to remove Castro and they were desperate to restart their lucrative gambling, drug and smuggling businesses in Havana.

Kennedy was far more important to them than Castro and they needed him alive if the CIA was to carry out any future coup in Cuba. With Castro out of the way, they could resume operations.

A second link to organised crime was uncovered by investigator Stephen Rivele in the 1980s however (he would later write the screenplay for Oliver Stone's *Nixon*). It aired as a documentary by a British production team called *The Men Who Killed Kennedy* and it was initially snapped up by the American networks. Rivele interviewed Frenchman Christian David who was already incarcerated in an American prison for drug offences. David claimed to have been offered the Kennedy contract but he turned it down

Far Right: *David named Lucien Sarti as one of Kennedy's killers*

as too risky when he learned it was to take place in the United States. Instead, the job was taken by three Corsican hit men: Lucien Sarti, a reckless killer and drug trafficker; Roger Bocagnani; and Sauveur Pironti. (David only mentioned Sarti and refused to name the other two.)

In the autumn of 1963, the three men flew to Mexico City before crossing the border into the United States on Italian passports. They drove to a safe house in Dallas run by the Mafia so that there could be no record of them in the country. They then photographed Dealey Plaza and decided on trapping Kennedy in a crossfire using three weapons. David went on to suggest that two of the snipers would take up positions in buildings behind the motorcade – with one high up (in the book depository) and the other on the horizontal (the second floor of the Dal-Tex building) – while the third man would fire from the knoll. All three would be wearing uniforms to blend in with the security personnel in the plaza.

The men fired four shots, of which two occurred almost simultaneously: the first struck Kennedy in the back; the second struck Governor Connally; the third killed the president; and the fourth

missed, hitting the curb and injuring James Tague. In the confusion, the three men were able to return to the safe house, where they remained for ten days. They then flew from Dallas to Montreal, and from there returned to Marseille.

Rivele was intrigued by David's story, but it would remain just that unless he could find someone to substantiate it. David suggested he try tracking down Michel Nicoli, a narcotics dealer turned government informant who was now a federally protected witness. In June 1986 Rivele finally convinced a DEA official to lead him to Nicoli. The Frenchman was known as an expert and reliable witness and he confirmed David's story. Rivele then returned to David, now in prison in Paris, and gave him the names of the other two assassins.

David confirmed that he had the right men and then said that Sarti had wanted to be on the railroad bridge but that it was guarded. This part of the story checks out as two policemen were patrolling the top of the underpass on the morning of the shooting. Sarti instead chose the grassy knoll as it offered an equally good vantage point. According to both David and Nicoli, Sarti used a frangible or dum-dum round to fire the

Right: *Mourners at the British embassy in London signing the book of condolence for the assassinated Senator Robert Kennedy*

fatal shot.

But Rivele's exhaustive three-year investigation also begins to unravel at this point. He asserts that Carlos Marcello placed the contract with his contact in Marseille, Antoine Guerini, and that the three men had ties with the Chicago Mafia. When Rivele took his case to the DEA officer and the FBI, they said that he needed two credible witnesses to testify before it could be brought before a grand jury, but, although Nicoli agreed, Christian David refused until freed from prison.

Pironti stated beyond doubt that Sarti was in Baumettes Prison in Marseille and Bocagnani was imprisoned in Bordeaux at the time of the assassination. Another assertion was that the three men had fired four shots from three different positions, the shots striking Kennedy and Connally in the back coming from separate buildings, and the fatal shot definitely coming from the front. This could not explain how three spent shell casings that had definitely been fired recently could be found in the book depository. The French government then provided the documentary's maker, Nigel Turner, with solid alibis for two of the men and Rivele's case fell apart.

Fidel Castro

FIDEL CASTRO

Far Right:
Fidel Castro is questioned after the attack on the Moncada Barracks

Castro was presiding over a Communist government that was allied with the Soviet Union. From 1959 he oversaw the import of Russian nuclear missiles that were soon pointing at the United States. When American U-2 spy planes discovered the missile sites matters came to a head during the Cuban Missile Crisis. It was no secret that the Eisenhower and Kennedy administrations were concerned about the threat and were determined to remove Castro via a variety of measures, some peaceful and legitimate, others illicit and overtly aggressive.

Castro had taken an unorthodox route to power. Born the illegitimate son of a wealthy farmer, he attended the University of Havana and absorbed anti-imperialist left-wing politics. He was soon making a name for himself as a revolutionary and helped fight the right-wing governments in Colombia and the Dominican Republic. He then turned his attention to organising a coup against the pro-American Cuban junta of President Fulgencio Batista. Batista was a corrupt politician who allowed American casinos run by the Mafia to spring up across the island, particularly in Havana. Castro was appalled at the influx of crime bosses and the increased corruption so in 1953 he launched an attack on the Moncada military barracks at Oriente. He was captured and imprisoned, however.

Above: *Raúl Castro with Che Guevara*

Far Right: *Castro (right) enters Havana in 1959*

more effective ways of removing him from power and allocated a $13 million budget to the CIA to employ the Mafia to carry out the change of leadership. The Mafia were only too pleased to be asked because Castro had boycotted or closed down the majority of their gambling interests on the island.

In September 1960, Castro flew to New York for the United Nations General Assembly. He refused to stay in an upmarket hotel and instead highlighted the inadequacies of a country so rich it couldn't help the poor, oppressed and persecuted people in areas like Harlem. He found Soviet Premier Nikita Krushchev especially sympathetic and the two developed a strong relationship.

Having attended a Fair Play for Cuba dinner, Castro headed back to Havana, but he was concerned that a US-backed coup was ready to take power. He spent $120 million on Soviet weapons and had soon doubled the size of his army, and he also recruited a vast civilian militia. By January 1961, Castro was convinced that most of the staff at the US embassy were spies and that a coup was imminent so he sent the majority back to America. The response from a

Having been released the following year, he joined his brother Raúl in Mexico, and the pair teamed up with Che Guevara to overthrow Batista in the 1959 Cuban Revolution. They then nationalised American interests and formed an alliance with the Soviet Union. This so alarmed Eisenhower that he ordered an economic blockade of the island, which included banning the import of Cuban sugar, but the measure was ineffective and Castro only accumulated power by standing firm against American heavy-handedness.

Eisenhower was forced to look at

newly elected Kennedy in Washington was to cut all diplomatic ties with Cuba and remain the master of its own house. The CIA also increased its support for Cuban exiles and asked them to attack ships trading with Castro to disrupt the island's economy.

Kennedy then modified Eisenhower's invasion plans and armed 1,400 dissidents. They sailed from Nicaragua while eight B-26s bombed airfields inland. Castro was incensed and placed his forces on high alert, but they did not anticipate an amphibious landing at the Bay of Pigs and the coast was poorly defended. The CIA had hoped that the rebels on the island would now rise up and overthrow Castro but many defected, allowing Castro to launch an immediate and effective counteroffensive. Kennedy refused to step in and help the rebels and abandoned them to Castro. The Cuban leader then paraded the captives and interrogated them on live television. It was a triumph for Castro and a disaster for Kennedy and tension between the pair ratcheted up another notch.

The following year, with his country's economy in decline, Castro was asked by Krushchev if he could

deploy medium-range ballistic missiles in Cuba. Castro reluctantly agreed, partly because he believed it would guarantee his country's security and partly because building the silos would create jobs.

U-2 spy planes picked out the launch sites before the missiles had arrived. With the discovery of Soviet nuclear bases only 90 miles from the Florida coast, Kennedy was forced to consider ordering Castro's assassination rather than simply trying to overthrow him. But he first ordered that all ships approaching Cuba should be searched under strict quarantine conditions. (He didn't know then that more than a hundred missiles were already in place on the island.)

Castro countered by urging Krushchev to threaten a nuclear strike in the US if Cuba was attacked again.

Right: *President Kennedy tries to resolve the crisis with Soviet Foreign Minister Andrei Gromyko in the Oval Office in October 1962*

The Soviet premier was desperate to avoid war, however, and began secret negotiations with Kennedy to remove American missiles in Turkey and Italy in exchange for withdrawing the Cuban missiles. The deal was done and war was averted at a late stage but Castro, who had been preparing for a second invasion, heard about it on the radio and was furious that it had been struck behind his back. This weakened Castro's position so he demanded that the US end its embargo, stop its support for the counter-revolution and withdraw from Guantanamo Bay. Kennedy refused. Castro countered by denying UN inspection teams entry into Cuba. Tension between the pair was at an all-time high.

Kennedy then appointed his brother, Robert, the attorney general, to oversee Castro's elimination. The CIA embarked on another program of recruiting Cuban exiles and Mafia hit men as spies to infiltrate the Cuban government and to help with its covert raids in the hope that Castro could be at the very least usurped from power.

Castro hit back again in September 1963 by saying that if the United States continued to target him and his country, their leaders would not be safe from retaliation. After the assassination two months later, the Warren Commission barely mentioned a possible link between Oswald and a country and leader he admired, and made even less of the Kennedy administration's determination to oust Castro from Cuba. Nor was the commission told that Castro's was not an empty threat, so the public was not given the facts about his motive.

President Johnson publicly supported the commission's findings but he was privately convinced that Castro had used Oswald to get to Kennedy before the CIA had got to Castro. The Watergate scandal and the secrecy surrounding the Vietnam War only fuelled the fire because now the American people had solid proof that their government had lied to them. Then the CIA plots to kill Castro also became public knowledge and further undermined the Warren Commission.

In the mid-1970s the House Select Committee on Assassinations re-examined the evidence and even visited Castro in Havana to confront him. G Robert Blakey suggested to the Cuban president that he might have been involved in the assassination but Castro denied the accusation with a strong argument: it would have given the US the perfect excuse to invade Cuba with an all-out assault, something he had worked his entire life to avoid.

On balance, it is certainly possible that Castro ordered Kennedy's assassination: after all, it was no secret that Kennedy was trying to eliminate the Cuban leader under the codename Operation Mongoose, and this provides him with a strong motive. The means was Oswald, the opportunity Dallas. But the reality was quite different. Having forced Krushchev into backing down during the missile crisis, Kennedy's advisors urged him to force home his advantage and strike another blow to Communism by building bridges with Castro. Kennedy liked the idea but needed a go-between who would appeal to the Cuban leader.

Former soap star and then ABC personality interviewer Lisa Howard had made her reputation by being granted audiences – some of them impromptu, such as that with Nikita Krushchev in Vienna – with world leaders like Kennedy. She had set her sights on interviewing Fidel Castro in the aftermath of the missile crisis, but he had so far refused to meet her. With both men agreeing to her involvement, she was finally granted a televised interview in April 1963. When broadcast, it garnered political acclaim and gave Howard a platform from which to further her interest in Castro and his relationship with the US.

Kennedy then granted her permission to speak with Cuban Ambassador Carlos Lechuga at her apartment. American diplomat William Attwood was also invited, and it was his remit to approach Lechuga and smooth relations with Cuba. On the back of this introduction, Attwood was invited to meet Castro in Havana in December 1963, with Howard acting as intermediary.

Kennedy then invited reporter Jean Daniel to the White House as he knew the Frenchman was on his way to interview Castro. Kennedy briefed him in the Oval Office to extend an olive branch to the Cuban in the hope that Castro would extend the same courtesy when he returned. On November 19th, Kennedy made a speech in Miami that promised better relations with Cuba if Castro stopped promoting subversion throughout Latin America and severed his ties with the Soviet Union. Kennedy left for Dallas hoping that there would be news from Castro on his return to Washington.

On November 22nd Jean Daniel met Castro and delivered Kennedy's message. Castro was enthusiastic about a warming of the relationship because he was disappointed with the involvement of the Russians. During lunch, Castro took a phone call and was given the terrible news from Dallas. He was mortified and confided in Daniel that the world would think he was responsible. He also knew it was the end of the peace mission because Lyndon Johnson would have to be seen to take a tougher stance against Communism.

Left: *Lisa Howard with Fidel Castro*

Lisa Howard interviewed Lechuga a few days later and he confirmed that the opportunity had been lost to stabilise Latin America and develop the Cuban relationship with the US. Lyndon Johnson didn't want to pursue the dialogue in case he was accused of being weak by the republicans in the lead-up to an election, so it seemed the negotiations were dead in the water.

Howard, however, still had access to Castro. In a subsequent interview, she asked if he would continue to negotiate with the new American president. Castro agreed so they drafted a letter to Johnson asking him to renew talks, but enthusiasm in Washington had cooled further and Howard was asked to end her relationship with Castro. The Cuban was bitterly disappointed because had Kennedy not been assassinated, he believed a second term would have allowed the president to lift the embargo and renew diplomatic talks.

The Russians

There are essentially two theories about Soviet involvement in the Kennedy assassination, the first being that the KGB carried out the shooting, and the second that they hired or coerced Oswald into pulling the trigger.

The US government was extremely suspicious of the Soviet regime in the early 1960s and they were worried that a possible first strike against America would involve removing the president and vice-president. (This was why Lyndon Johnson was so eager to board Air Force One in the aftermath of the assassination because he believed he was also a target for a Communist conspiracy originating in Moscow. He also ordered US forces the world over to be placed on high alert in case they had to shoot down incoming missiles.)

It had already been reported that Oswald had been in Mexico City two months before the assassination. He visited the Russian Embassy claiming that his life was being made unbearable by the FBI surveillance and that he wanted another visa to return to the Soviet Union. His application was denied so, despite wishing to travel to Cuba, he returned instead to the US. This is the official version, and it was given by Oleg Nechiporenko, one of the diplomats who interviewed Oswald. But it doesn't tally with the stories given by Pavel Yatskov and Valeri Kostikov who were also present. All

THE RUSSIANS

Above: *Valeri Kostikov*

(In 1993 Nechiporenko released a book called *Passport to Assassination* in which he concluded that Oswald killed JFK because of his extreme feelings of inadequacy conflicted with his wife's admiration for the president, and that the KGB never tried to recruit him or extract sensitive information from him.)

Kennedy had successfully stood up to the Russians during the Cuban Missile Crisis of October 1962 but this angered and humiliated the Soviet leadership. Whether Nikita Krushchev knew of a plot to target Kennedy or if a hard-line Stalinist element went behind his back isn't clear but the theory goes that the hardliners wanted nuclear war with the Americans, or at the very least they wanted to force Kennedy to back down.

A ruthless but brilliant spy called Ivan Serov had overseen the displacement and liquidation of enemies of the state during the Second World War. Krushchev appointed him head of the KGB in 1954 and head of military intelligence (the GRU) five years later. Serov had powerful allies in the shape of Yuri Andropov and Vladimir Kryuchkov, and many believe it was these three who planned

three have since been outed as members of the KGB. Indeed, according to the CIA, Kostikov specialised in sabotage and assassination.

the assassination.

Serov contacted Kostikov through the KGB system and may even have been able to convince him that the assassination was officially sanctioned by the Kremlin. Indeed, many have asked why a man of so little importance like Oswald would have been granted an audience in Mexico with Kostikov and two other senior diplomats. The real reason may have been that Oswald was either already in their employ or was about to be recruited for the assassination. Either way, he certainly wasn't the nobody everyone thought. The theory gained credibility when it emerged that the 'diplomats' sent a telegram to Moscow immediately after the meeting.

J Edgar Hoover passed President Johnson information on Oswald in the weeks before the assassination, convincing the latter that the Soviets were behind a plot to kill Kennedy. When he heard that Oswald had lived in Russia, was under FBI surveillance and had tried to enter Cuba, Johnson was appalled, and this information naturally reinforced his opinion that there was a conspiracy to assassinate the president.

Robert Holmes, author of *Spy*

Like No Other, believes that of all the conspiracy theories this one is the most likely as it is credible, easily implementable and fits with all the circumstantial and forensic evidence. Oswald carried out the shooting alone but he was working for a rogue agent within the KGB.

If Oswald was not involved and had been framed for the shooting, however, was it possible that KGB agents carried out the assassination? There is no doubt that Krushchev had been humiliated when Kennedy forced him to back down during the missile crisis, but was this a powerful enough motive to kill the president? The Warren Commission didn't believe there was a shred of evidence implicating the Russians, but recently released files do hint at the KGB targeting other international leaders.

In the aftermath of the assassination, Lieutenant-General Ion Mihai Pacepa defected to the West. He was the highest-ranked Soviet intelligence agent to reach the US and he claimed to have had conversations with Nicolae Ceaușescu about the KGB's assassination programs. Ceaușescu believed that the Kremlin had targeted, amongst others,

Imre Nagy in Hungary, Gheorghui-Dej in Romania, Jan Masaryk in Czechoslovakia, the Shah of Iran, Mao Tse-tung and President Kennedy.

Pacepa gave additional detail on the latter two attempts, claiming that Mao would be removed with the help of Chinese Communist military leader Lin Biao, and that the KGB had meticulously planned the assassination of John F Kennedy. However, in a later book, *Programmed to Kill: Lee Harvey Oswald, the Soviet KGB, and the Kennedy Assassination*, released in 2007, he conceded that Oswald pulled the trigger.

Although there will always be proponents of the Soviet conspiracy, and it does seem the most plausible given Oswald's connections with the country and his self-professed Marxism, the motivation continues to prove the major stumbling block. Kennedy may have embarrassed Krushchev the year before, but the reality was the two men respected one another and neither wanted to see another crisis develop into nuclear war. A first strike by the Russians at Kennedy could have provoked that war, something both men were desperate to avoid.

Left: *Yuri Andropov*

Far Left: *Mao Tse Tung, Chinese Communist leader*

The CIA and the FBI

In 2003, a poll in America showed that nearly a fifth of the population believed Vice-President Lyndon Johnson and the country's security services were involved in the Kennedy assassination. It was no secret that there was a healthy dislike between Kennedy and Johnson because the vice-president believed Kennedy was going to drop him in the build-up to the 1964 election.

Joachim Joesten's 1968 book *The Dark Side of Lyndon Baines Johnson* accused Johnson and the Dallas oligarchy, along with members of the security services, of plotting the assassination. Fellow researcher Barr McClellan alleged in his 2003 book *Blood, Money & Power* that Johnson also needed to cover up various

scandals, and that oilmen worried about Kennedy changing the oil depletion allowance and costing them $100 million paid Johnson's associate Malcolm Wallace to fire at the motorcade from the sixth floor of the depository. Indeed, one of the partial fingerprints found in the sniper's nest apparently belonged to Wallace even though he'd never been in the building.

Documentary maker Nigel Turner (*The Men Who Killed Kennedy*) used this theory as part of his ongoing investigation, calling the episode *The Guilty Men*, but there was a fierce rebuttal from Gerald Ford, Jimmy Carter and a host of presidential aides. The History Channel, which had aired the film, was

Left: *CIA operative E Howard Hunt was rumoured to be one of the three tramps in Dealey Plaza*

forced to apologise and withdrew the series when it found the facts did not fit the theory.

However, a woman called Madeline Brown then came forward saying that she'd been Johnson's mistress and that he *had* been involved with the assassination. She claimed that he'd been looking for the right opportunity to remove Kennedy after the president had repeatedly embarrassed him, and that Johnson had been at a meeting of the conspirators at oilman Clint Murchison's house on November 21st 1963, the night before the assassination. Her story appeared again in the 2006 documentary *Evidence of Revision* and was corroborated by several of Johnson's associates.

Even Doctor Charles Crenshaw, who had tried in vain to save Kennedy at Parkland Hospital, and who had also tried to resuscitate Oswald, suggested that Johnson at the very least wanted details of the assassination covered up. He said that Johnson had called the trauma room in the hope of extracting a full confession from Oswald because the president wanted a concerned America to think he'd acted alone, with Castro as the next to be accused if the public didn't buy the Oswald story. Crenshaw was forced to tell Johnson that Oswald was in no condition to give a statement.

If Johnson really was involved, it's likely he would have recruited the security services to help plan the

assassination. It was no secret that President Kennedy and the CIA also did not see eye to eye on a number of issues, particularly those surrounding political assassinations. The agency openly assisted the Vietnamese when Lucien Conein murdered President Diem. Kennedy was shocked at what the agency had done and was quoted as saying he wanted to splinter the CIA into a thousand pieces and scatter it to the winds. Journalist Arthur Krock believed the writing was now on the wall. He suggested that the agency was spreading like a cancer and was becoming too powerful and therefore unaccountable. He even mentioned the possibility of the CIA launching a coup against Kennedy.

After the disastrous Bay of Pigs invasion, Kennedy blamed the CIA for a lack of intelligence and their inability to convince the Cubans that Castro needed to be removed. Kennedy and his brother Robert felt there was a general atmosphere of distrust between them and the agency and they sacked Allen Dulles, its head man, in 1961. Johnson could barely disguise his hatred of Kennedy and there's little doubt the two men didn't get on, so the conspiracy theorists argue that Johnson organised the hit so

he could assume the presidency while the CIA would remain well-funded and allowed to continue its covert operations.

The theorists identified three tramps in the plaza as E Howard Hunt, a CIA station chief who apparently gave a deathbed confession over his and Johnson's involvement in 2007; CIA agent Frank Sturgis, who was also involved in the Bay of Pigs invasion and

Above: *Frank Sturgis and Tramp B were supposed to be one and the same person*

who was said by Marita Lorenz to be one of the gunmen; and Chauncey Holt, a man claiming to be a double agent for both the CIA and the Mafia. Hunt also claimed Agent David Morales and an unnamed French assassin were involved,

the latter firing at the motorcade from the grassy knoll.

Photos of the three tramps show them bearing a surprising resemblance to Hunt, Sturgis and Holt but the Rockefeller Commission was quick to point out that the men who had made the comparisons, assassination researchers Alan Weberman and Michael Canfield, had no formal training in photographic identification and that the FBI's internationally renowned department of photo-identification and analysis concluded that none of the tramps was Hunt or Sturgis. The House Select Committee on Assassinations also examined the pictures and concluded that none of them bore any anthropomorphic resemblance either to the agents or to Thomas Vallee, Daniel Carswell or Fred Lee Crisman, all of whom had been named by conspiracy theorists as potential gunmen.

The three tramps theory can be definitively discounted when the evidence is closely examined: Hunt was in Washington on the day of the assassination, and this was confirmed by his family and employees. The Dallas Police Department's records back this up: the tramps were arrested shortly after the shooting in the railroad yard but they were determined to be Gus Abrams, Harold Doyle and John Gedney. They were held for several days before being released without charge. Hunt's apparent confession was made, according to his widow, when he was extremely ill and rarely lucid by two of his sons who were motivated purely by greed.

The evidence against Johnson, the CIA and the FBI is barely credible. Although Kennedy had a number of disagreements with the agency, Deputy Director John Hegerson felt that their relationship was better than that which had been nurtured under Eisenhower. CIA official William Colby thought the pairing with the Kennedy administration reaped countless benefits because the president understood the agency and its intellectual value, and it helped him analyse and assess the political and military landscape at home and abroad.

The accusations levelled at Johnson in particular are unfounded. The new president was actually convinced that Castro was responsible but that he was powerless to act in case tension with the Soviet Union escalated and led to nuclear war. So although Johnson wasn't involved, he did try to cover up what he believed was the truth about Castro's part in the shooting. His biographer, Robert Caro, found no evidence from his exhaustive research that Johnson had any involvement in the assassination, a fact that conspiracy theorists tend to overlook having not done the research themselves.

The Other Theories

Some researchers point to the assassination having been planned by members of the New Orleans underworld. Immediately after the shooting, Attorney Dean Andrews told the FBI (and later the Warren Commission) that he'd received a call from a Clay Bertrand asking him to defend Oswald. Several more witnesses then came forward to say that private investigator Guy Banister and employee David Ferrie were both working for lawyer G Wray Gill on behalf of Mafia boss Carlos Marcello.

In what would become the basis for Oliver Stone's 1991 film *JFK*, District Attorney Jim Garrison investigated the New Orleans connections and concluded that Ferrie and Banister had been convinced by local businessman Clay Shaw – who used the pseudonym Bertrand – to carry out the assassination and then frame Oswald. In March 1967 Garrison arrested Shaw and put him on trial for the murder (the only person ever to be brought to trial in the case), although the jury found him not guilty.

Other conspiracy theorists believe that because Kennedy was looking to withdraw from Vietnam, which would have seriously impacted on the profits of the arms' manufacturers, defence contractors and the Pentagon's budget, a military-industrial complex of these factions conspired to eliminate the president. There's no doubt that Kennedy was exploring peaceful

options, both in Vietnam and with the Soviet Union, so a coup d'état from within the services is not an unreasonable suggestion, but future presidents also looked for ways out of Vietnam and for a cooling of the Cold War. A coup would surely mean a complete change in policy from the new leader, which did not happen after the assassination.

In 1959 Castro swept to power in Cuba and many people left the island to live in the United States. A movement began to coalesce with the sole intention of returning to Cuba and overthrowing Castro but their hopes were dashed when the botched Bay of Pigs invasion only strengthened Castro's position. This so angered the Cuban exiles living in the US and they blamed Kennedy for the loss of their homeland. They believed that Lyndon Johnson would take a much tougher stance against Castro, and he would be more likely to continue using the CIA to try to assassinate the Cuban leader. Kennedy,

Above: *Clay Shaw was the only man to be tried for his part in the assassination*

Right: *Two American soldiers waiting for the second wave to come in during the Vietnam war.*

therefore, needed to be eliminated.

The House Select Committee on Assassinations was receptive to the idea that anti-Castro Cubans might have been involved. In 1979 they reported that Kennedy's popularity among the exiles had plunged by 1963, and a tape-recording of a meeting between exile Nestor Castellanos and far-right Americans in Dallas just before the assassination points to a plot: "We're waiting for Kennedy on the 22nd. We're going to give him the works when he gets to Dallas. I wouldn't even call him President Kennedy." The HSCA concluded that although the anti-Castro Cubans as a group were not responsible, one or two members may have been involved. It also hinted that far-right conservatives angry with Kennedy for backing Martin Luther King and promoting racial equality also might have been involved on the basis of the meeting with Castellanos, but it afforded this theory much less weight and little attention is given to it today.

In his book *Crossfire*, Jim Marrs claims that Kennedy was trying to limit the power of the Federal Reserve. He believed that executive order 11110 would transfer that power from the reserve to the treasury by replacing notes with silver certificates. A conspiracy of the ultra-rich and power brokers then allied with the CIA to remove Kennedy.

This theory stumbles at the first hurdle, however: Kennedy actually signed legislation increasing the power of the Federal Reserve over the treasury by advocating notes over the proposed certificates. And the executive order was a temporary measure only to be used in times of transition or for administrative convenience.

Although there are a host of further conspiracy theories, the last one with any credibility at all involves Zionist Israelis who believed Kennedy was attempting to thwart their production of nuclear weapons. Israeli Prime Minister David Ben-Gurion and the country's security services, Mossad, were supposed to have planned the assassination with help from Lyndon Johnson and the CIA. In a speech before the General Assembly of the United Nations in 2009, Libyan leader Muammar Gaddafi also alleged that Kennedy was killed in response to him wanting to investigate the nuclear power station at Dimona. In the final analysis, this seems like just another theory that has little substantiated evidence behind it.

Analysis of the Photo & Video Evidence

As the motorcade approached Dealey Plaza, Robert Hughes filmed the cars from the corner of Main and Houston. He used his 8mm camera to film the crowd and then the president as the motorcade turned onto Houston. His film shows the open window on the sixth floor of the school book depository but he stops filming as the motorcade turns onto Elm Street. Had he carried on for a couple more seconds, he might have caught the sniper leaning out of the window and shooting at the president, but his film stops as soon as the car is out of sight. Although Hughes may not have captured images that could have thrown more light on the case, several witnesses did see a man fire at the motorcade from

the book depository.

Orville Nix started filming from almost the same spot as Hughes but he crossed the plaza as the motorcade turned onto Elm Street and filmed the assassination on his 8mm Keystone camera from opposite the grassy knoll. Although he was some distance from the motorcade, his camera did pick out the entire knoll and stockade fence during the shooting. But the relatively primitive camera with indoor instead of outdoor film and no correcting filter doesn't give much detail of who or what is on the knoll. Had he loaded the correct film, more details of the knoll would have been revealed.

Charles Bronson also caught part of

the assassination on his still and video cameras. The blurry still coincided with the first shot, which he identified as a gunshot, so he immediately began filming. He only snapped two seconds of footage before the fatal shot struck Kennedy. The motorcade then disappeared behind the trees. It's difficult to glean much from either his still or video shots, however.

Jim and Tina Towner filmed the motorcade from the corner of Houston and Elm but they both stopped filming when Kennedy was out of sight. Moments later, the shooting started. Tina would later help trace the missing first bullet because she distinctly remembered the car passing beneath the traffic lights below the sixth floor of the book depository.

Above: *Phil Willis's photo clearly shows the grassy knoll behind the presidential limousine*

Phil Willis had a still camera, which he used to take several shots of the motorcade coming down Main Street. He then ran to the corner of Houston and Elm and took a picture of the cars as they headed towards the Stemmons Freeway sign. The shot only captures the back of the presidential limousine but it does reveal all of the grassy knoll. At first glance, there doesn't appear to be anyone on the knoll.

Mary Ann Moorman had a new Polaroid Highlander 80A camera and she was also opposite the knoll. Her picture

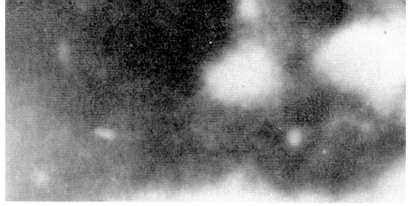

was taken within a sixth of a second of the fatal shot to the president's head, and it gives a clear view of the knoll, but it too fails to pick out a potential shooter, unless the conspiracy theorists' 'Badge Man' hypothesis is believed.

The theory states that a gunman wearing a police uniform was behind the stockade fence on the grassy knoll, and that he can be seen in the Moorman picture. Part of his face is obscured by what the conspiracy theorists claim is the explosive discharge of a rifle round. But the people in the original photo on other parts of the knoll are relatively easy to distinguish, whereas the supposed badge-man area is indistinct and so underexposed that it cannot answer the question of whether a gunman is behind the stockade fence.

When the theorists apply their photographic techniques and add colour to the image, a person appearing to fire a weapon gradually materialises (although no facial features are discernible). However, the theory is eventually dispelled when the figure's size is calculated relative to the height of the five-foot retaining wall and the other people in the picture. For Badge Man to be a real person, he would be less than three feet tall according to Doctor Lenny Rudin at Cognitech who has repeatedly analysed the image. Either that or he was standing on top of a twenty-foot scaffold in the railroad yard forty feet behind the fence, which is clearly unreasonable as he would have been seen by hundreds of people, including Lee Bowers in the railroad tower.

This also calls into question Gordon Arnold's testimony, even though he

Right: *If colour is added to the image, even more appears*

believes he can be seen in the Moorman photograph. His claim that he recorded the shooting on a cine camera that was then confiscated by Badge Man is unfounded and likely untrue, and this is again backed up by the size of the supposed figures and that Abraham Zapruder was filming only yards away and saw nothing of this supposed interaction. In fact the only person who claimed to see a man hit the ground as the shots were fired – as Arnold said he did – was Senator Ralph Yarborough in the second car behind the presidential limousine. But Yarborough would not have been able to see behind the wall from his position, so his testimony too lacks credibility.

It is a sad truth that some publicity seekers and mentally unstable individuals

are desperate to become part of history. In many of the photographs of the assassination a woman wearing a headscarf can be seen filming the action only a few yards from Mary Ann Moorman. Investigators have tried for half a century to track her down, with no luck. Every so often someone will turn up claiming to be the so-called Babushka Lady, such as Beverley Oliver. But Oliver's story has changed many times over the years – she initially claimed to have filmed the assassination on a Super 8 Yashica Camera but it wasn't sold in the US for another two years – and she even claimed to have met Oswald (who was working for the CIA of course) with Ruby two weeks before the assassination. When a big part of someone's story turns out to be false, their remaining testimony

Above:
Zapruder's camera is now in the national archives

landmark photo, it will probably never yield more about who could have been on the knoll. It's worth noting that none of the Secret Service agents in the cars saw anything unusual on the knoll during the assassination.

Mary Muchmore's film also captures the bank leading up to the picket fence, but it doesn't reveal any more than postal worker Mark Bell's footage, which was also shot from opposite the knoll. His images do show people running towards the knoll in the aftermath of the shooting, however, although no gunman can be discerned from his footage either.

The most famous footage of the assassination was shot by Abraham Zapruder, who worked in the Dal-Tex building on the plaza as a dressmaker. He was standing on a concrete pedestal on the bank overlooking the motorcade route to the west of the book depository. He was filming with an 8mm Bell & Howell camera with a zoom lens and Kodachrome II film.

The Zapruder film contains 486 frames, corresponding to 26.6 seconds of footage at 18.3 frames per second. After the assassination, Zapruder volunteered his camera to the Secret Service so the film could be examined in detail.

cannot be replied upon. Arnold's story, too, has changed many times over the years and cannot be trusted.

Unsolved History recreated Moorman's picture on the 40th anniversary of the shooting and compared it with the original. The Moorman picture was not as distinct, and, although it remains a

Eastman Kodak's Dallas office processed the images and the Jamieson Film Company produced three copies. Two were given to the investigative teams but media interest was so great that a bidding war erupted over the final copy. *Life* magazine eventually beat off competition from CBS and paid $150,000 for it, although Zapruder insisted that frame 313 – the fatal headshot – should not be published. (Although it was always believed that Zapruder had captured the shooting in its entirety, recent evidence about the missed first shot suggest it may have already been fired while he was not filming and that his footage is of the assassination once it has already started.)

In 1991, Oliver Stone paid the Zapruder family $85,000 to use the footage in the film *JFK* and the government eventually paid the family $16 million in 1999 because it had

been designated an official assassination record. As of 1999, the copyright is owned by the Sixth Floor Museum in the book depository.

The film intrigues us because it shows a good portion of the shooting. The Stemmons Freeway sign probably hides the moment when Kennedy was first struck, however, and if Zapruder had turned another few feet to his right as the motorcade accelerated towards Parkland Hospital he would have captured the stockade fence on the knoll by the triple underpass and may have answered questions about who, if anyone, was there.

Amateur camerawoman Elsie Dorman was filming from the fourth floor of the book depository but her shaky footage initially yielded little. However, she claimed that she stopped

312

filming immediately after she heard the first shot. Her testimony has intrigued investigators ever since because the motorcade had only just rounded the corner onto Elm Street at this point, which is much earlier in the timeline than people believed the first shot was fired. Eyewitness Amos Euins agreed with Dorman, however, in that the first shot was fired while the motorcade was passing beneath a set of traffic lights by the corner. This traffic pole would become central to the investigation 50 years later because a new team concluded that the first bullet might have struck it, which would explain the missed shot when the president was only around 100 feet (30 metres) away, a much easier shot than that which eventually killed him.

The photographic evidence is

Above: A fraction of a second before the fatal head shot

inconclusive because although it answers several questions it asks even more. It does, however, help tidy up a few loose ends: conspiracy theorists have long argued that the bullet hole in the president's jacket doesn't correspond with the autopsy report of where the bullet struck him. (This also affects the supposed trajectory of the magic bullet, of which more below.) In several of the pictures Kennedy's jacket and its collar are bunched, which explains the discrepancy.

In 1979 the House Select Committee on Assassinations was about to deliver its report having re-examined the evidence. Lead investigator G Robert Blakey knew that science and technology had advanced in the intervening 15 years but, having trawled through all the autopsy photographs, witness statements and reams of evidence from the KGB, CIA and FBI, he remained convinced that Oswald alone had pulled the trigger.

However, just before his report was due to be delivered, three scientists concluded that audio evidence gleaned from an open police microphone confirmed that there had in fact been two gunmen in the plaza. Although the recording was of poor quality, their analysis appeared to prove that three

shots came from the book depository and one came from the grassy knoll. Two shooters meant there had indeed been a conspiracy to assassinate the president, and, having being a staunch advocate of the lone gunman theory, Blakey now became a believer in the conspiracy.

But there were problems with the scientific evidence: the microphone had to be on the corner of Houston and Elm when the first shot was fired,

for example. The motorcycle policeman whose microphone apparently captured the shooting, H B McLain, was also unconvinced the recording had come from his machine because sounds on the dictabelt tape did not match his recollection of events. Sirens were not heard for two minutes after the shooting, whereas his had been blaring all the way to the hospital; the sirens that were heard exhibit the Doppler Effect suggesting

ANALYSIS OF THE PHOTO AND VIDEO ANALYSIS

Right: *For the dictabelt evidence to have any chance of being valid H B McLain's motorcycle microphone needed to be in the pink circle on the corner of Houston and Elm but he had only just turned onto Houston Street*

the microphone was stationary; the motorcycle itself sounds like a three-wheeler; there's no crowd noise heard during the first part of the journey down Main Street; the gunshots can't be picked out by the human ear; a voice says "Hold everything secure" at the point where the shooting was supposed to be happening; and someone is heard whistling a minute after the assassination.

The final nail in the dictabelt evidence came from McLain himself because he claimed his motorcycle wasn't even in the plaza during the shooting. His claim is backed up by the photographic and video evidence, which suggest he was as much as half a block behind the limousine.

The committee's findings were rejected in 1982, with the likely source of the recording being a three-wheeled motorcycle at the Dallas Trade Mart on the route to Parkland Hospital. The motorcade passed this spot with sirens blaring, which explains the Doppler Effect; the officer on the motorcycle was known for his whistling; and Sheriff Bill Decker's 'hold everything secure' quote was made about a minute after the shooting. All of this evidence points to a different microphone to H B McLain's being the source of the recording.

RELATIVE PO

The Single Bullet Theory

One of the most contentious issues surrounding the assassination involves the bullets themselves. How many were fired, from where did they originate, and who or what did they hit? Most witnesses in the plaza – including Governor Connally who was an experienced hunter – counted three shots, and all of the initial news reports agreed with him. The majority of people interviewed afterwards also stated that there was a noticeable pause after the first shot, while the last two were much closer together. (In all, 132 of 178 witnesses, an overwhelming majority, said they heard exactly three shots.)

This gives rise to several different theories about the shooting, one of which (the official Warren Commission version) states that the first shot missed, while the second shot struck Kennedy in the upper back and, having passed through his body, then caused all the injuries to Connally in the seat in front. This is known as the single bullet theory. The third bullet then struck Kennedy in the head. The first shot, which the commission said missed the motorcade, has never been satisfactorily accounted for.

A rival theory states that the initial injury to Kennedy and the wounds to Connally could not have been caused by the same bullet as the two men don't appear to react at the same time on the

CE 399

FBI C1

National Archives

Zapruder film. This has given rise to the magic bullet theory, magic because it apparently entered too low in Kennedy's back to exit his throat, then waited in mid-air before striking Connally in the back and changing course several times to inflict all of his injuries. There's little doubt that the third shot struck Kennedy in the head, but some argue that it might have happened at exactly the same time as a fourth shot was fired from the grassy knoll.

The Warren Commission eventually decided that the evidence supporting a single bullet strike to both Kennedy's upper torso and Connally's back was persuasive, but they hadn't initially reached this conclusion. When examining the Zapruder film, which had a frame speed of 18.3 per second, they concluded that Kennedy first reacted to the impact of a bullet between frames 225 and 226. Connally, on the other hand, didn't seem to react until around frame 235. Ten frames of the film corresponded to only just over half a second, clearly nowhere near enough time for the shooter to reload, aim and fire accurately. The FBI had already tested the rifle and concluded that it took at least 2.3 seconds (42 frames)

to recycle the weapon. They therefore agreed with the commission's initial findings that there must have been at least two snipers in the plaza.

The doubters know that the single bullet theory is central to the Warren Commission's account of the assassination, and the reason is based on the timing of the shots. President Kennedy was waving to the crowd and did not appear to have been hit by the time the limousine passed behind the Stemmons Freeway sign at Zapruder frame 205, but we know he was clutching his throat by the time the car reappeared from behind the sign at frame 225.

This narrows down the timing of the first shot to hit him. Connally is definitely struck by frame 240, which, even if frame 206 is taken as the time when Kennedy was first hit, doesn't give a single sniper enough time (1.86 seconds) to recycle, aim and fire the rifle. This time can be refined further because there was a tree in the way of a shot from the depository until frame 210, and closer examination of the Zapruder film shows Connally reacting by frame 235.

However, when the FBI re-enacted

Far Left: *The 'magic' bullet in the national archives*

the shooting in May 1964 they found that because of the actual positions of the seats in the car, the injury trajectories through the president and Connally's bodies aligned very closely, providing the bullet had been fired between frames 207 and 240 when Connally's body was in the right position. They also found that with practice the rifle could actually be recycled in a little less than two seconds. Robert Frazier, one of the FBI's weapons experts, eventually managed to fire three accurate shots in only 4.5 seconds. (A second recreation of the shooting in 1978 revealed that the echoes around the plaza made it quite difficult for witnesses to pinpoint the origin of the shots, which helps explain the diversity reported on the day itself.)

Three agents found the single impact theory improbable because of the relatively pristine condition of the bullet when it was found on Connally's hospital gurney, even though the bullet was matched to the rifle found in the book depository by forensic and ballistic tests to the exclusion of all other weapons. Connally and his wife Nellie also disputed the theory because they believed that Kennedy was struck in the upper back by the first shot before the governor himself was hit by the second. But they also both agreed that Oswald was the lone gunman, which doesn't fit the timing of the shots on the Zapruder film because no one could have reloaded in such a short time.

As any high-powered rifle bullet striking both men would have taken less than a hundredth of a second to pass between them, it's hard to explain why both men initially don't appear to react at the same time. The conspiracy theorists believe this is incontrovertible evidence that there must have been more than one gunman, despite the forensic evidence pointing to the bullets coming from the Carcano in the depository.

Some believe that the fatal shot was fired from a storm drain in the pavement on Elm Street in front of the limousine, but when *Unsolved History* tried to recreate the shot from this position, the president wouldn't even have been visible. More people suggest that shots came from the drains on top of the triple underpass or from the plaza's southern knoll. The south end of the underpass can immediately be ruled out because the drain hadn't been installed by November 1963, and there was no

direct line of sight to Kennedy for the fatal shot. The same is true from the knoll. The north side of the underpass offered a shot at the president's head but there were trees and people in the line of fire and a sniper would have been unlikely to have fired from this position. Railroad employees on the underpass were all interviewed after the shooting and they insisted they saw no one and nothing unusual. This rules out the triple underpass as a vantage point for a sniper.

The second floor of the Dal-Tex

building was also named as a potential vantage point but, when the presidential limousine was at the position of the two shots that definitely struck the occupants, there was no direct route to Connally's back, meaning the single bullet theory from the book depository was infinitely more likely than a 'magic' bullet from elsewhere.

On balance, the ballistic evidence suggests that the first shot from the depository probably occurred earlier than most people thought (when Zapruder wasn't filming). Because it missed, what happened to it remained a mystery until a new investigation into the shooting by Max Holland in 2011 discovered that it almost certainly struck the traffic light assembly above the corner of Houston and Elm (a hole can be seen in the lights in the FBI's photographs of the crime scene) and that it disintegrated and ricocheted down the street where fragments struck the curb and injured James Tague. One spent shell casing was found in a different place to the other two in the sniper's nest, which indicates that the shooter probably shifted position having fired the first shot. The sniper would have been panning the weapon

across the plaza and may not have realized immediately that the shot had hit the light assembly. A short period of confusion could have explained the apparent pause of around six seconds between the first and second shots.

Although this view is challenged by computer animator Dale Meyers, who believes Zapruder captured the entire sequence of shots (with the first being fired at frame 160) and whose exacting CGI representation of the shooting based on all the available video and photographic evidence won him an Emmy Award, it seems inconceivable that an experienced marksman who was able to deliver two accurate shots at a much greater distance could have missed not only the occupants but the entire car at a range of no more than 100 feet (30 metres).

The second shot was probably fired at Zapruder frame 221. It exited the Carcano with a muzzle velocity of around 1,900 feet per second (580m/s) and travelled 189 feet (58m) before striking Kennedy two inches to the right of his spine in his upper back. It then damaged his first thoracic vertebra, passed through his neck and exited his throat just below his Adam's apple. It then began tumbling before striking Governor Connally below his right armpit, destroying five inches (127mm) of his fifth right rib, passing through his chest and exiting below his right nipple (frame 223).

Indeed Meyers's analysis shows the lapel on Connally's jacket puffing out in this frame so he concluded that this was when the bullet exited the governor's chest. A couple of frames later both the governor and Kennedy react in unison to the impact of a single bullet, much earlier in Connally's case than had previously been believed. Still travelling at about 900f/s (274m/s), it then entered and exited his wrist, breaking the radius before lodging shallowly in his thigh. When he was undressed in the hospital, the bullet was dislodged and was found on the stretcher.

Opponents of the single bullet theory still refuse to accept that the bullet could be in such good condition having done so much damage, but tests done at the time by the Warren Commission and many more since have proved that these bullets *can* survive with only slight flattening when they hit skin layers and ballistics gel, as well as when they strike harder substances like wood and bone.

There was plenty of action within the car in the following seconds as Jackie and Nellie tried to shield their husbands from the marksman. Connally tried to turn to check on Kennedy but he was already injured and rolled back and to the left.

The third, fatal, shot hit Kennedy at frame 313, or approximately five seconds after the second shot. The sniper therefore probably had as much as 11 seconds in which to take the three shots, and maybe a little bit more, not the six seconds (or fewer) claimed by most conspiracy theorists.

Although it appears that Kennedy's head is snapped back and to the left, Meyers's exacting animation shows his head initially moving forward by up to two inches (five cm). When the side of Kennedy's skull blows out from the impact, his head then rolls to the left. This is again consistent with a shot from the rear, not from the front as the physics of the impact (the skull blow out causes an equal and opposite reaction) and a stiffening of the body due to massive nerve damage do contribute to a secondary movement to the left rear. A re-enactment by British sniper Michael Yardley for the

program *Unsolved History: Inside the Target Car* replicated the results with a shot from the position of the sixth floor window in the depository. Yardley also found that a shot from the front right would have passed through Kennedy's head and struck Jackie, which clearly did not happen.

The program's findings were backed up by two eyewitnesses at the hospital. Before the Secret Service started cleaning the car, which was unusual given that it was a crime scene, student Jack McNairy saw inside the limousine. Motorcycle rider H B McLain then arrived to help Jacqueline out, and he also saw important forensic details from the car. They both agreed that the blood and brain matter was mostly on the back of the front seats and along the limousine's right hand side, which was consistent with a shot from the right rear.

The Physical Evidence

There are many conspiracy theories surrounding JFK's autopsy. The official version is that having examined the clothing, photographs and X-rays, the autopsy physicians at Bethesda Naval Hospital in Washington described entrance wounds in Kennedy's back at the base of his neck just above the shoulder blade, and a second to the rear of the head.

They didn't attempt to track or dissect the neck wound because they were unaware that the bullet had exited his throat at the front (the exit wound had been obscured by the emergency tracheotomy performed by doctors at Parkland Memorial Hospital earlier that day).

The fatal wound to the president's head could be tracked via minute fragments of the bullet from the small entrance hole in the back of his head. The impact dislodged a roughly palm-sized portion of the skull, leaving a ragged exit wound at the front of the head.

The Warren Commission and a number of later studies (the Rockefeller Commission and the House Select Committee on Assassinations) concluded that the president had been struck by only two bullets, both of which were fired from behind, above and slightly to the right. The bullet from the fatal shot fragmented, with one portion contributing to the blow out of the

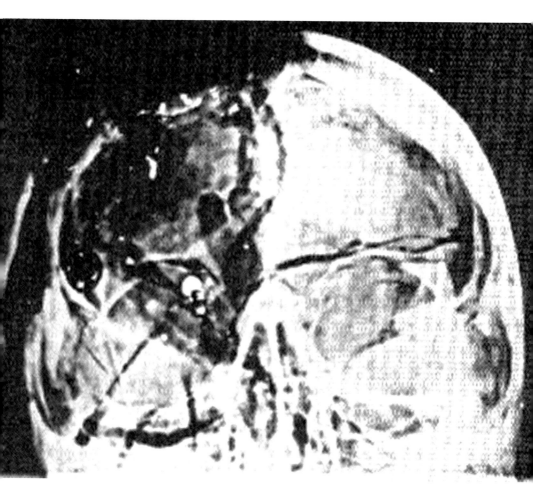

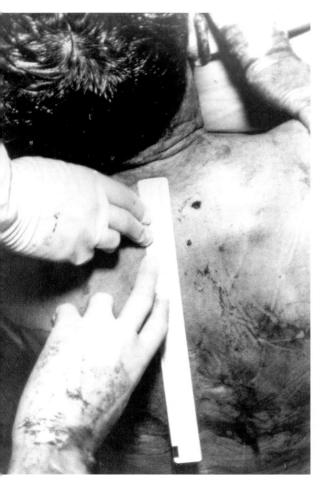

right hand side of the skull. There was no damage to the left hand side of Kennedy's head, which eliminated the possibility of a bullet striking from the front right. Any bullet entering from here would almost certainly have struck Jackie or the car afterwards but neither was hit. The only trajectory possible for this bullet was back to front from above and behind the motorcade.

The conspiracy theorists argue that standard protocols were not adhered to, however. Kennedy's autopsy should have been carried out by Doctor Earl Rose at Parkland but the Secret Service overruled him and removed the body illegally. Also, Doctor Paul Peters and Doctor Robert McClelland believed that because the damage to the rear of the skull was so great, and that around 20% of the brain was missing, the fatal shot might have come from the front. The autopsy photograph of the rear of the president's head shows the small entrance hole, however.

Because there was still so much speculation about the assassination, the HSCA's 1979 report also looked at whether the autopsy records – photos, X-rays, medical notes – were genuine and if they could have been altered in any way. Having examined the files in great detail, the forensic anthropologists studying the case had no hesitation in stating that the files were genuine and that they had not been altered. Photographic scientists and radiologists agreed that the images had not been manipulated and that the committee's forensic pathology team had come to the correct conclusions about the assassination. They all believed that there was no evidence of a gunshot wound from the front and that if there had been the chance of it leaving no trace was extremely remote. The discrepancy between the doctors' testimonies and the autopsy photos is easily explained: the technicians in the photo are pulling the skull fragments – held together by skin and tissue – back into place to reveal the entry wound. The damage to the side of the skull is still clearly visible.

With such weight and credibility behind them, most people accepted the autopsy reports, but a minority highlighted several inconsistencies in the examination of Kennedy's body: the HCSA criticised the Bethesda technicians for not describing the entry wounds accurately and leaving the autopsy report incomplete with regards to photos, X-rays and their notes.

The release of the Oliver Stone film *JFK* in 1991 only reignited interest in the assassination and drew attention to the autopsy itself. In response to the public outcry, Congress created the Assassination Records Review Board to collect and analyse the assassination records and to ensure they were placed in the National Archives where they would be available to the public. Congress did not want another full-scale investigation into the shooting but it was happy for the ARRB to clarify the medical evidence and present the facts.

The ARRB's chief analyst, Douglas Horne, was expected to deliver an uncontroversial report on the autopsy findings but he claimed that the photos of the president's brain were not of Kennedy; the first examination's pictures were not included in the official record; the second examination included fraudulent photos; the pattern of damage to the skull was inconsistent to what had been reported by doctors at Parkland Hospital; and the subsequent autopsy at Bethesda highlighted more differences from those noted by doctors in Dallas.

Doctor Gary Aguilar believed Horne and went on record saying that the brain that was re-examined had a large frontal

Far Left: *The entrance wound in Kennedy's upper back*

Original Motion
Picture Soundtrack

PRESIDENT KENNEDY
DEATH BY ASSASSIN I
SHOT TO
DALLAS

AN OLIVER STONE FILM

JFK

Music Composed and Conducted by
John Williams

exit wound consistent with a shot from the rear, but that this was not Kennedy's brain as his had a large exit wound at the rear of the skull, which, because it provided more evidence of a shot from the front, was not released to the public.

However, since the photos from the autopsy are readily available, and almost all of the experts who have examined them believe them to be real and unaltered, it is difficult to side with the conspiracy theorists. The entry wounds to the president's back and to the rear of the skull, the blow-out on the right hand side of the head above the ear and the X-rays provide conclusive evidence that Kennedy was struck twice, with one bullet passing through his back and exiting his throat, and the second entering the rear of his head. Both were fired from the sixth floor of the Texas School Book Depository.

Above: Governor Connally's jump-seat is clearly much lower than the rear seats. It is also several inches inboard

Far Left: A poster for the controversial Oliver Stone film

Conclusion

There is no doubt that the Kennedy assassination will divide opinion for the foreseeable future. Although some of the conspiracy theories raise important points, most are not based on demonstrable fact, solid science or the overwhelming circumstantial and forensic evidence. The Oliver Stone film is a classic case in point.

Stone suggests that there were a number of sinister happenings in New Orleans, including David Ferrie's 'confession', Oswald printing Fair Play for Cuba leaflets and then handing them out while Clay Shaw looks on, and Richard Helms admitting that Shaw worked for the CIA. Stone, unfortunately, did not base any of these incidents on real events: Ferrie never confessed and always denied any knowledge of Oswald or the assassination plot; the leaflets Oswald handed out were not printed by him; and Helms never claimed that Shaw worked for the CIA.

Stone also took liberties with the events themselves, as well as the witness reports from Dealey Plaza: he puts Kennedy and Connally in seats that are the same height and alignment, but Connally was sitting in a lowered inboard jump-seat that was completely offset from the president's; he has Jackie pulling Kennedy down into the car to make way for the shot that hits Connally, but this does not happen in

JFK **CONSPIRACIES**

the Zapruder film; the entry wound in Kennedy's back and the exit wound in his neck are incorrectly positioned; a cloud of smoke appears on the grassy knoll, but no one reported this; Jim Garrison (played by Kevin Costner) claims that 51 people heard shots from the knoll but even the advocates of the many theories have managed to identify only around 30, and most reports put the number at fewer than 20; in the film, Bill Newman says the shots came from the stockade fence on the knoll, whereas he actually believed the shots came from the mall behind him; it's claimed that if the sniper was Oswald, he couldn't have fired the last shot, stashed the rifle and been seen 90 seconds later in the lunchroom completely unflustered, but the trip through the depository only takes half that time at walking pace; and Lyndon Johnson apparently asks for the limo filled with bullet holes to be refurbished, but the bullet strike to the windshield and chrome are in the national archives. (This list of factual inaccuracies is nowhere near exhaustive.)

The film reignited interest in the event itself and the plethora of conspiracies surrounding it, but Stone's version of events is not supported by the facts and simply bombards the viewer with alternative explanations, none of which seem credible after further examination. So although it is certainly possible that there were three or more snipers in the plaza, and it's equally possible that the mob, Russians, Cubans or intelligence agencies were somehow involved, it's much more likely that Oswald alone was responsible. This is what the facts and not the Hollywood misinterpretation or the conspiracy theories suggest.

It is always the case with incidences like these – the death of Princess Diana, 9/11, the Moon Landings, UFOs – that there will be some aspects of a case that are not easily explained. The truth seems to be that mistakes are made during the investigations, and conspiracy theorists then cite these inaccuracies or unintentional oversights as evidence of sinister goings on. Every time the conspiracies are debunked the theorists come up with an alternative explanation until they end up with such an implausible scenario that they change tack. A classic example of this is the conspiracy theorists citing the Zapruder film as inaccurate or an elaborate hoax, or that the limo stopped to give the shooter a better chance of hitting Kennedy. Both of these assertions are demonstrably false, so the theorists have to modify their claims and try again. (Other questions like why the Zapruder film would be altered to omit the car stopping or to conceal or reveal evidence are difficult for the theorists to address. None of the other films of the assassination show the car stopping, so their credibility is undermined once more. As usual, they move on, claiming that Secret Service Agent William Greer, who was at the wheel of the presidential limo, turned and shot Kennedy point blank in the head or neck with a pistol, which is again demonstrably false when the videos are closely analysed. And none of the occupants of the car reported this either.)

Also, how is it possible for a government to keep evidence suppressed or kill off all the important witnesses without someone blowing the whistle? It's impossible for politicians to keep secrets for more than a few minutes so how could the

enormous number of people required by each theory manage to keep quiet for half a century? No single credible NASA witness, for example (or any of the thousands of people who worked on the Apollo missions around the world), has ever claimed the Moon landings were faked, and the same is true for the JFK assassination: no alternative has stood up to detailed analysis by credible investigators.

Why couldn't a disillusioned and mentally unstable man have ordered a rifle, taken it to work and shot someone? Just because that person was the most powerful man on Earth and he was supposed to be protected by the Secret Service doesn't necessarily mean that a huge conspiracy was involved in the assassination. We want there to be equilibrium, with the president and his entourage on one side, and the killer with backing from a vast network on the other because then the events seem more plausible, but it's perfectly possible for Oswald to have acted alone and the vast majority of the evidence backs this up. His brother, Robert, knew Oswald better than anyone, and he has always maintained Lee's guilt, and that he acted alone.

CONCLUSION

Right: *John F Kennedy*

As inquisitive humans, we like to find patterns where perhaps there are none. We like to question official versions of events because there will always be some who don't believe what they are told. These are natural reactions – our governments have lied to us before. We find it very difficult to believe that one man could do so much harm to a country and shatter people's beliefs in their own security. But the fact remains that Oswald had the means, motive and opportunity to carry out the assassination, and it was he who pulled the trigger.

It is also highly unlikely that he was working for the mob, the Russians or Castro, or indeed any domestic organisation such as the CIA or the FBI. The most likely to have recruited him would have been the Russians – this requires the smallest leap of faith because he did at least have documented Soviet connections – but Krushchev and the KGB were as anxious as Kennedy to avoid war and a direct strike at the President of the United States could have led to a nuclear holocaust. So, the most likely scenario is that Oswald, a bitter, unhappy and unstable man, was the lone gunman.

JOHN FITZGE

1917

124

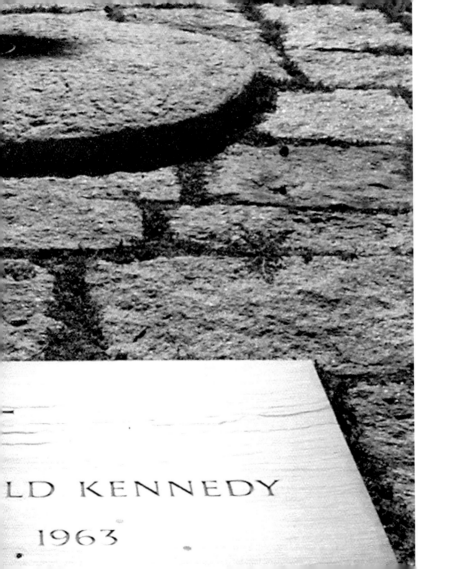

ALSO AVAILABLE IN THE LITTLE BOOK SERIES

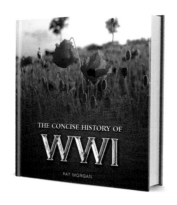

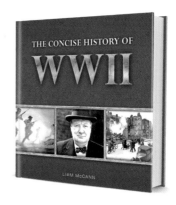

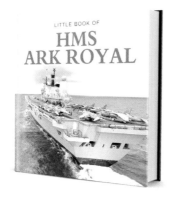

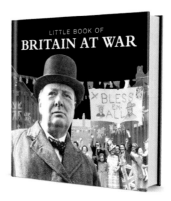

ALSO AVAILABLE IN THE LITTLE BOOK SERIES

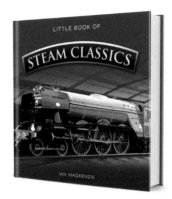

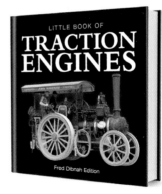

The pictures in this book were provided courtesy of the following:

WIKIMEDIA COMMONS

Design & Artwork: SCOTT GIARNESE

Published by: DEMAND MEDIA LIMITED & G2 ENTERTAINMENT LIMITED

Publishers: JASON FENWICK & JULES GAMMOND

Written by: LIAM McCANN